MW00721037

Mine

STEPHEN COLLIS

New Star Books

Vancouver

2001

New Star Books Ltd.
107 - 3477 Commercial Street
Vancouver, BC   V5N 4E8
www.NewStarBooks.com
info@NewStarBooks.com

Cover by Rayola Graphic Design
Typesetting by New Star Books
Printed and bound in Canada by AGMV-Marquis Imprimeur
1 2 3 4 5   05 04 03 02 01

Publication of this work is made possible by grants from the Canada Council, the British Columbia Arts Council, and the Department of Canadian Heritage Book Publishing Industry Development Program.

Le Conseil des Arts | The Canada Council
du Canada | for the Arts

BRITISH
COLUMBIA
ARTS COUNCIL

NATIONAL LIBRARY OF CANADA CATALOGUING IN PUBLICATION DATA

Collis, Stephen, 1965—
  Mine

  Poems.
  ISBN 0-921586-87-6

  I. Title.
PS8555.04938M56 2001   C811'.54   C2001-911330-7
PR9199.3.C633M56 2001

For Cathy,

for my parents,

for all our ancestors,

and for the coal miners of Vancouver Island

Mine

Tailings: Anthromite

Maydays in August

polytrope

sun fall on sugar maples

inseparable

conglomerate

revolutions

the house turns

on its dream

mechanism

fortunate

to view its other

astral regions

opening

the dark

whelm

Going

fertilizer

acquisitions

embargoed

coal productions

the soil

cat like contorts

leaves of

the Dominion

beholden

to dust mite

Arcadian

discourses

To test

the memory's

gain in

registers

unfold

the sporadic

donators

of phosphorus

bespectacle

the morning

unshine

in western

celestial woods

That angels

rebel

why not miners

the course of

thermodynamics

how electors elect

vicissitudes

light

stains

the lawn with

shadows

out thrown

by mercury

coal dust and

loci imagines

An import

protrudes

rheumatic arrows

on screens

unleaven

the debriefing

circumstantial stone

fortitude

in forests

the cat stalks

photosynthesis's

agro-memory

yawning

corporate

gains

Shaft

One

Two Origins as Opening Utopiana

I

Making   their mineral sojourn   stone time hot & humid
plants fell & died where they fell   thickly layered with woody
remains compresst   over aeons becoming layered rock & sand
compresst   becoming layered in stone   plant memory or the
carbon thereof   transformed into coal   bright ideas awaiting
interbanded with other rock layers

Elsewhere   time an engine   a weary foe or pithecoid
ancestor detaching a nodule of flint from a chalk bank   the rock
layers bent & broken by the winter seed of forgetting (our priceless
gift)   compresst in its slow coming   scoured & scraped the
face of the land the memory of earlier vegetative life forced in
revolutions of subterranean blood & dynasty

Over time   green thoughts rekindle   coming up from
compresst depths to clothe the glaciated land   so only sea
carving revealed pale granular sandstone   dark & crumbling
shale   shiny black coal

Intruded upon (by) nature   from the dawn the digging of
ores   thunders   the great discard   the rocks disclose
flint-napping   bison soon drawn in black outline like dried
flowers presst between the pages of an old album (although nature
has no writing and our human words   are intrusions) the
savagery of unregenerate man

II

The rocks under your feet (dear myriad) provide little pre-history
lies jumbled in the geological forces   the variations we may see
in our hardly perceptible lifetime

Back to the time (Oceania) of the Island's rocks   the story nearly
striking dramatic beauty & pebble rocks from a location somewhere
off California   drifted northward one centimetre per
year   generated this geo/logical collis/ion buckled elevating
mountains a broad basin

A mild repository (we think: time, a rock) climate forest & swamp-
land eroded these materials (synapse)   underlie the vegetation
deposited & compresst (superego)   near-vocal coal (grammar!)
deposits (material!)   & hyphenated prosperity unending

This great geo/logical standoff   after a quiet period of further
erosion   tremendous rivers of ice flowed merciless to converge
with time & residues in thick lowlands   cropping sediment
scraped & carried away pushing & finally retreating from fields of
gouges & grooves   (groves compresst)   glacial erratics of
granite & granodiorite

Happily   black dream uplifting earth began its slow rebound
fragments announced emerged from beneath the sea (geo time
scale)   the Gabriola Formation & the Benson Formation
exposed rock surfaces (to sleep) come from near the bottom strata
signifying sediments & unexpected survival of the words for them

The Newcastle & Douglas seams ancestral rock older stretching
recondite from Nanaimo Shaft Point towards McKay Point
although the delineation & naming of these layers copper sodality
came much later opening doors onto adventure & distrust

Thus ochery output of firms formed the ancient formation faults
crossing (pneumatic & grammatological drill machinery)
passage & vent creating the faulting process (layers shifting into
colonized shafts) a second fault line functioning   distance (no
treaty for mineral rights) (stone text & porcelain parvenu)   a
scarp drops Dr. James Hector to the beach examining coal
structures *circa* 1860   to whit:

The Preface

This place where light
floods in upon shadows

while the poem pools
before the ungainly architectures
of the page

      opine   tumescent   arche

arch
upon
arch

the lines   Gothic
lift a rhetoric
of stone into the preface

a portent of confusion

an archaic form of gossip

a glowering towards the reader

a prince of first words kingdoms

'No one said it would be easy
and this was really not (luminous)
after all the author's (apartment)
intention and if you (dear reader)
think I had in any way (fabliau)
contrived to amend the (discursive)
ocular scope of eternity's (flounce)
own unsullied sorting chamber (manteau)
then you most certainly have (acrobatically)
misread me all together'

A

polished

space

left

for entrance

and carousel

she

bade

the preface

begin

This

word's

ochery

horn blast

turns

in the amber

of its own

muted

mesmerism

a small

antechamber

opening onto

a garden

justifying

the text

beyond itself

The preface
begins
     to recollect
          the shape
of remembering

architecture and memory
a mezzanine overlooking

What is the architecture of mines?
What is their memory?

Inversion
whispers into absence:

'the other is lovelier
than anything else you can imagine'

There is an Art of Memory

explaining
the carnal presence of certain facts
not yet in evidence

not yet spoken
in the spent penumbra of pretext

not yet a novitiate
of fake Latin epigraphs

The kindling spirit

even translated

from language of leaf light

to black stone

is present

ignites

is not forgotten   To whit:

is the not forgetting   as Mnemosyne

is memory, geologic   stands over the poem

                                                          as memory igniter

                                                        so the Coal Queen

                                                     stands ready to spark

                                                              the ore of a

                                                               geopoetics

Wherefore   the preface is
that which is laid down and buried beneath
the reading that comes in its wake

is the foundation of archeology shadowed
beneath the present city's day dreaming

is the memory of text awaiting
exploitation
and upturned layers of textual echo
and fire foretold
in the dark of words crushed into unmeaning

is the unmeaning of memory
awaiting the fire of being re-read

fold upon fold in
unnatural light of meadows

Thus the preface is book memory speaking
before its foliate self glows

is time twisted

is prophecy's masquerade ball

is words' amber and ambient armature
glinting fronds of once and future foretellings

'as the light of his candle
played across the tumble of
magnificent artifacts'

walking out of the dark
and into her painting.

Of the Poem's Chiaroscuro

How to remember dismembered histories, memories crushed under the collapse of time? Propose that mining involves an Art of Memory, accesses the 'memory table' (*c.f.* the geologic water table). Following veins of black ore into labyrinthine underground galleries, reaching towards the deeper ore horizon, the miners burrow into pure earth memory, petrified tree recollection. The pick flies at the foliated rock and birds flutter from forgotten branches, the sound of wings beating deep beneath the ground; the coal lump cracks red and throbbing in the grate and cedar sparks lift up, the scent of a Haida ceremonial chest having just been opened to retrieve.

From the most ancient times the covering and uncovering of the earth. 'In just such a way a miner when he has descended and left the *light* of day and of life far behind, if ever the roof trembles and the earth above gives way with a sudden crash, lies forever hidden, buried beneath the *dark* avalanche, and his body, broken and crushed far within the earth, does not release his chafing spirit to the stars' (Statius, *The Thebiad*). Some paragons of the ancient Art of Memory were said to have carried several whole buildings full of images around in their heads — think what networks of mine tunnels and shafts the miners must have born in their memories, anti-architectures of inverted night and day spaces, faces black with coal, heads adorned with fish oil fires, images of day life freely associated and arranged in the dark unconscious expansive and Heraclitean around them. Dreams of rebirth, of the Phoenix, the new arrangement of data in *speculum, tabula, synopsis, methodus, encyclopedia*, of Persephone returned from Hades' black grasp.

Historians, supposedly in the business of cultural memory, form painterly *chiaroscuros* of time's shifts. In the nineteenth century John Ruskin imagines architecture's luminaristic benefits: a tower 'would bring *light* into the eyes to see from afar, lifting its fair height above the *dusky* purple crowd of humble roofs.' His SEVEN LAMPS OF ARCHITECTURE attempts to lift the brilliance of eternal verities above the contingent squalor of Blake's dark satanic mills. 'There is occasionally a burst upwards and a blossoming unrestrainably to the sky . . . adding a general enrichment to the deep shadows that relieve the shafts.' With this last word the dark of the century's mines also come to the fore, a shadow my imagination adds to Ruskin's. 'We may feel that a massy shaft and a bold shadow would be worth it all. Nevertheless . . . if its points of *shade* and *light* tell in general effect, we shall not be offended by finding that the sculptor in his fullness of fancy has chosen to give much more than these mere points of light.' Architecture, according to Ruskin, is indispensable to memory, as it was to the ancient Art of Memory: 'We may live without her, and worship without her, but we cannot remember without her. . . . There are but two strong conquerors of the forgetfulness of men, Poetry and Architecture.'

The nineteenth century also saw coal become 'The torch bearer of civilization.' One can read across the terrible inventions, bridging worlds, placing new memory images in old colonial *loci*.

1815: miner's safety lamp invented (if rarely used).
1823: Champolion deciphers hieroglyphics.
1825: Brunel builds the first tunnel under the Thames.
1834: the first trade unions are founded. Braille invents printing for
the blind.

All these, in the dark time shaft. Memory, *chiaroscuro*, are also technologies, inventions, set somewhere in the dark contours beneath our feet.

My family came piecemeal to this seacoast edge where East meets West, unsettling rather than settling, by the turn of the century, shopkeepers and for the most part coal miners. Nanaimo, Wellington, Cumberland — places given new memories. Most of the mines are closing by the 1930s, after no more than sixty years of operation. Generations die quickly, without passing their stories on. I have a few, others in my family have their own — pieces of the

smoldering stone. But little is recorded: we were not a family that
kept written records. The civic archives are only hollow reminders
of what is missing — the unwritten lives of the poor and history-less.

Know them by what is missing, the scars and imperfections of
memory. This is their story. I mine it as I write it. I imagine its
chiaroscuro patterns. Two images stand out from the dark behind.
One a woman, who came seeing and painting. The other a miner
alone in the pit, lightless and cold after a collapse or explosion in
the catacomb shafts beneath Nanaimo's harbour. I see him most
clearly in the light and shadow brush strokes of her paint, assisting
his return. Two pictures hung in *Memoria's* hall, withstanding the
architectural collapse of time. This alone to go on.

Shaft

Two

Tailings: A Glossary of Mining Terms

Alluvial	Aqueous	Agencies	
Air stack	Arch	Arch	
Bearers	Bifurcated	Bit	
Bituminous	Black jack	Black sand	
Blind shaft	(Winze)	Blue stone	
Bore hole	(calcinating pyrites)		
Canary ore	Cleavage	Conglomerate	
Crab holes	(Paleozoic country accidents)		
Cross spur	(generally basaltic humps)		
Deadwork	Divide	Dolly	Drift
Drop shaft	Face	False bottom	
Fault	Flat shaft	Flouting	
(containing sulphides, antimony or lead)			
Flume	Footway	Fossicker	
(to the miner as is the gleaner to the reaper)			
Fuse	Gain	Gash vein	
Grey ore	Ground sluice	Harrow	
Head wall	High reef	Hole	
Hopper	Jumper	Kibble	
(see Whim bucket)		Knocker	
Ladder road	Life	Lode	
Main shaft	Mill	Miner's rights	
Monkey shaft	(as a rule perpendicularly)		

Mullock	Pall	Pawn	Permit
Picker	Pillar	Pinch	Pit
Plutonic	(deep seated igneous forces)		
Pocket	Prop	Reef worker	
Riddle	Rope rider	Rock	
Scove ore	Skid shaft	Sludge	
Softplate	Spentshot	Spur	
Strip shaft	Stull	Tailings	
(detritus)	Tailings machine	Tailings	
pit	Tormentor	(tub & spade)	
Tributer	Truck	Underlay	
Vein	Wallplates	(hanging wall)	(hole)
Warden	Water hole	Water shaft	Weight
Whim bucket	Windbone	Winze	
(for ventilation)	(the undefinable)		

From swamp
to coal seam

       rock layers we
          re bent
        & bro
           ken —

*This   when primitive man   an otherwise solid barrier of up
folded Cretaceous strata   seeking stones   porous dreams of
infidels   fashioning fears into a fetish   this habit of heritage and
more malleable metals   the glint of it picked up as divinities
beneath the water summoning such stones an ornament   small
lump along stream edge hammered into useful purpose   this
(stolen) (text) of Western decoration   their bare arms encircled a
measure of value in the form of rare coins found amongst Chaldean
ruins   nothing but nature's supplies and fire   a lexicon of hard
mineral words   dark and unburnished as forest fires told by
Lucretius sound   this mortal action of shepherds   employing
incendiarism*

Upper Cretaceous shales and sandstone of the Nanaimo Group
deposited just after the collision (of Wrangellia and Laurentia):

Haslam (shale)	*Extension* (conglomerate)
Pender (shale)	*Protection* (sandstone)
Cedar District (shale)	*De Courcy* (sandstone)
Northumberland (shale)	*Galiano* (conglomerate)

'Two kilometers thick   and gently inclined   to the east'

'folded and faulted'   with dark pockets of coal   seams shot

black throughout   'Some Cretaceous plant fossils can still be

collected from   the old slag heaps and mine dumps'

ancestors

grey

smoke

from a

coastal

cabin

'The mind seemed to grow giddy by looking so far into the abyss of time'

Excursus: Time's Blindshaft

What is sacred   a chorus
chanting   the sound

itself a solvency in echo
an intoning since

a bride's first principled footsteps
outgoing   as Émile watches

the picture unfolding   is bestial
and insulting to our dignity

as human beginnings   'So that I
must start with all the woes

(*Germinal*)   and fatalities which weigh
down on the miners'

acrobatic and insular   *Quoting is*
a mongrel technique

removing rock from scattered and
various textual layers

(of time) (Zola) the scientist   puts his
substances into contact

in a suitable container (environment)
(feeling a world out in echo)

and then plays no further part   this
physiological doom (family)

no point in foolish tub thumping
the mischief begins

with a mixture   of past and present
sorting stone in the screen

room of memory (not merely a
number of puppets dancing

to a political tune)   she is envious
of Naturalism's

light lingering in the dreary dark
of mines

It is not legible   but audible
all desire

is within ear-shot   sinking
a shred of utopia

to decipher slowly
is Naturalism

a language   and words as pure ore
a Naturalism?

listened to with close fascination
repository of the

social score   to the coal of
texts' dark veins unfolding

rekindled in light pressed fluid reality
remembering they were

once here
once labouring

The theme is pneumatic and has
crystals

drills towards the other
(gods) in the dark

finds light   formative
at the origins

finds no origins only
other coal

of time's clipped pressures
soars   a wind

above passengers   crossing
Atlantics in the earth

Émile   silent amongst them records
revolutionary zeal

whispered threats   organic
discontents

The story again   *Che-wech-i-kan*   'Coal Tyee'   at Fort
Victoria blacksmiths observed coal shoveled into the smith's fire
and noted   that there was plenty of such stone   where he
came from   *Snuneymuxw*   the bedrock of what becomes
Newcastle Island   in the sea carved cliffs   the protrusion of
black rock   barefoot and *with a walking stick*   'These discov-
eries changed the complexion of the quiet inlet   forever'

1833: Reports of Island coal reach William Fraser Tolmie holed up
     and shivering at Fort McLoughlin.
1834: The steamship *Beaver* is dispatched / comes back with coal.
1841: 'Vancouver Island, so far neglected, was about to join the
     world of commerce.'
1852: Joseph Pemberton charting at James Douglas's request marks
     Exit Passage, Newcastle Island, Coal Seam No. 5   sketches
     the dark layers

Rather like a fox   being sent to guard the chickens   the HBC
collecting at Native expense   'at least equal   to good Scotch
coal'   foreseeing a colony   'under the control   of a
private company'   reaching into islands forests soils with
someone else's hands   'a child's hastily constructed toy'   set
down in wilderness   darkness of trees encroaching   'for the
purposes of working coals' (Blanshard)   encroaching

Miners are brought out of Troon   (displaying an almost auto-
matic resistance to authority)   (good for their health) from
Staffordshire   ('Brierley Miners')   from England's 'Black
Belt'   'It was 12 ere we sailed and a very coarse night it was'
(John Muir)   the sea chopping black walls of water out towards
their cramped bodies

The one thing the company could not afford   was to be selective
so politics came with pickaxes and toiling muscle   and with the
arrival of the Muirs   the Ur-family of Island mining   strike
was an instant threat   resistance   independence
increased demands   all the levels of appropriations shifting like
stone strata over millennia   'no mention was made of the Indians
who owned the land'   yes who owned the land?

Emigrating miners brought class struggle with them   or class
struggle brought the miners   one death for each month at sea
then another going down, a drowning in dark shafts sunk in foreign
savage soil   tinkering and tapping beneath Nanaimo's harbour
floor   (a crosshatch of passages   both subterranean and
submarine)   you could hear ship's anchor chains overhead
in the mine shafts beneath the sea

DUNSMUIR   (the old man had peopled the darkness
    with untold sufferings)

    the only stars which rose up now were the nocturnal
fires flickering in the land of coastal coal
        'who walks in that tall flame'   (shaman)
        'who then does all this belong to?'
                        (the unfathomable darkness)

            I saw into my open chest
            And found there a dark cave within
            Painted with charcoal images
            Of animals that were my kin

            The 1854 census of Nanaimo found 151
    white residents, only one of whom was
            over the age of thirty.   A line of shadows
            tramping slowly through the blast hunched
    with anger so that mine manager Robinson
            wound up 'picking up a hammer and
            hitting McGregor on the head'   counting
    coup on the 'downtrodden'
                    contused rather than extensive
                    the first strike called and lost
                        in a downpour on the cold coast

DUNSMUIR   (the shaft yawning   deep before him) hating
the common working man   (so easy to vilify)   though once a
miner himself   stood out of time's gloom   into the lamp
light of text   banning worker's meetings unions socialism any
political annoyances and especially the underground machinations
of those 'who make a trade of agitation'

Acting according to his archetype   the incessant rumbling of tubs
of coal   the pit gulping down   mouthfuls of men rapacious or
just good business   like some Victorian nocturnal beast of
commerce   'you know, we could be in his shoes'   discovering
the Wellington Seam, October 1869   producing a black flood of
coal: 88,000 tons by 1878, 190,000 tons by 1881   buying it all
up   a railroad as useful as a fifth wheel   two million acres
miraculously containing all the Island's known coal reserves   'he
had the Island   in the palm of his hand'

Coal flakes lift up on wings of miner's ghosts   become ravens
raucous in the Garry oaks and eaves of Craigdarroch Castle   a
coal clatter of laughter   'I did not want it said that I banished
little children and women in cold winter days'   but it was said

Once again he found himself in a maze of stairs and
    dark passages
        in which the miner's bare feet made a flopping sound
like old slippers

      as stealthily
           the beast night
        swallowed

if the cable breaks
      there is the well of ladders climbed

Then   in the darkness of the pit   he was stunned and lost
    all sense of direction   (this happens too often)
      through a blaze of light   a vision of a cave
    with men moving about   And then the void again

      below ground
          She   burst out
      a general storm
         emptying
    a hall hewn
      and lit by
hurrying

    two good kilometres
      the miners separated
    black holes in time
        to the left of nothingness

   the rumbling
 growing in violence
    the earth thunder
on their heads
   the under black

trembling

The Dangers: roof fall   coal dust clogging lungs   violent
equipment in dark confined places   afterdamp   the gas
gathering in invisible pools   to canary yellow explosions at
sparks last gleamings   the confusion of subterranean languages
an inverted tower of babbling Chinese Italian Polish Scots
Nanaimo miners three times as likely to die beneath dark earth
as miners anywhere else in the Empire   the methods
'lagging far behind those of other countries'   here   'on this
distant fringe of the settled world'

'No Chinaman is allowed to be in a responsible position such as
attending a ventilation furnace etc.   whether he can speak
English or not'   Endemic of divisions such as the ubiquitous
Chinatown   Coontown (Cumberland) everytown   its races
down   'I can't tell you any funny stories about the mine 'cause
there was nothing funny about it'

One place was on fire and another was flooded   one burning for
years down in the mine   so gardeners dug up smoke in their
gardens   the other   the water filled veins of the earth's
charcoal body   spitting up black bile into Campbell Lake or
dark springs lifting bloated corpses into the street to tell

strata of shale   sparkling
with mica   and duller masses   sandstone spurs
   rippling   beneath their   pensive immigrating feet
brothers   (and sisters)   of other's languages

   passing each other
     into the darkness
           a
      long black serpent
    deep shadow
        stone fallen
   opened and closed

whose dark shapes
foraged every knot in timbers
their troubles not
understood by others

      nearly seven-hundred
     of them now toiling in
       this immense
         anthill
      burrowing the earth
     like worm-eaten wood

    an occasional gleam (*chiaroscuro*)
threw them into momentary relief   the shape of a sinewy
   arm   a wild   dirty   criminal   face
a face   they cannot place   the difference of

Coal Queen

A flight
       of stairs, Piranesi

arch
     over
archway, a room
with few walls   entrances

in which   dreaming
     the bearded woman
speaks
black skinned and small
the wisps of jet black whiskers
soft along her jaw

figures of formless Orientalism
othering me from within

nothing else   but the mirror
shattered in the night
the splinters on the bathroom floor
rushing back light
and the image
of my own whiskered face

shard
     after
shard
     shot back black

'Look a me   I'm half Scotch   quarter English   and a
quarter somethin' else no one knows   I'm married to a Finn got
half Finn kids and part English and part Scotch and part what ever'
or   'What's a malla Jim   (we called all of 'em Jim)   what's
a malla you no loadum car?'   hate and fear hidden behind
humour   the little defile defiled by the passing of ignorance into
an age of too much plenty for too few   though no excuse
ordinary enough

'With what trepidation   they first entered the cage to go below
ground where so many of their friends and relatives had died is not
recorded'   259 white workers   266 Chinese (Wellington
1881)   the reason for the shift   Robert Dunsmuir   is not
difficult to find   white miners paid $3-4 per day   Chinese (&
other others) $1-1.25   'wages on which white workers would
have starved'

Dunsmuir's #5 Pit at Wellington   January 24th 1888   'O
Christ, the mine's exploding!'   deafened and dazed groping
their way through the pitch black mine   brought to the surface
as bodies crushed or perfect   the Chinese who are blamed (68
of the 148 dead)   known only by a number   *unclean*
criminal   immoral opium users   prostitutes (the story goes,
the dark crush)   *a great cancer   the ubiquitous heathen*
what wonder   'the Chinese who forgets his celestial origins so
far as to descend to the bottomless pit of a coal mine'   the
Yellow Flood proclaimed   by the anti-Chinese union meeting at
Harmony Hall   head tax   low wage Dunsmuir undercutting
with a racial axe

Slag

Radical

       this

orbed

         beauty of words themselves
       chipping away at

                 novelty
      this
        will
      machine
           endurance of
               archeology

cuneiform
mortality
wells
silence
the
organ of
God's
novelty
swooning

unmistakably

resembles

anatomy
            exaggerated   Europe

                        figures
            fertility
                        a goddess specialist

approached

            extent

            forced   abandonment of

                        northern shafts

Scavenged

discovery

impressions   *Something Profound Happened*

Pavlov   Potent animal past
                                               surfaced
speculation   carved inside
                                               cave
family members
                               migration   Occident/Orient
small game   ivory

bone debris   horse   cross hatched
                               expertly
quarry
                               ocher markings   ocher
                               body

                               'to produce an item of
                               this
                                      standard'

                               'confirms the existence of
                               an aesthetic
                                       consciousness'

From the coal face
the rippers
tunnel
every moment

down
the timbers
pale rents
too weak
this splintered wood
under

suddenly

Étienne
twisted
struggled

movement
weighed
him
planting
the body

shoulders & haunches
down in this starless night

Shaft

of light

each word
turned

glittering
itself
a small sun

alone   in the dark
space   the ache of the

arc   language

occupies

Shaft
of brilliance

buckling
concordant
immaculati

flowing   still   unstuttered

that name
that thing
thought
hidden

broken true

Shaft
of light

Humming
the dark   soundless
the past
dropped

scintilla
on the dark face eye
less name less coal
miner mine not mine

dead

forgotten
staring up
forever

Emergent

Elemental, the wind
painting the bough's roar

dark eyes blinking
amidst the thousand fractures
            of light

pieces of sound
of Vesuvius burying Pompeii

'Nothing lasts forever'
the graffiti reads
nothing but the coal face grimace

and the jay's screech
on the transparent dome
noble amidst the clatter

arms outstretched reaching
from Vancouver to Regina

1935 and the camps of the
unemployed   *On-to-Ottawa*

venting   the field
releasing dark horses, a dark
chariot and   a dark rider

bearing the hopes of the
working class off

to the underworld, *per aspera
ad astra*

Your hand, the pool of
flowers, your hand on
            the box of Beauty

opening   sleep
and oil fires
and passion gone out
            like a lamp

Through the rough roads
      to the stars

the portents of the eclipse
of Pompeii eclipsed

sealed in ash and
grimacing excess —
a distillation of the elements

in the swimming pool –
the old man surrounded
by screams   and splashing

arms outstretched, eyes
closed, bald head almost

transparent, his memory
visible, working men marching

riding the train tops to
riot in Regina, the clatter

of wave and light all about him,
the water opening   to release

the vision of Persephone
returned from the open earth

Beauty released from the
box of sleep

and the blue of his song
swimming up out of the green boughs
                once again

Shaft

Three

Tailings: Euphoria

In this discourse the most extreme flaws
into a field where
you walk
ushering daylight towards dusk
how I took you from the field
I knew not the poetics of
placing qualms where malaria hymns
and in facile time as incipient cod hunt
the insolvent souls I collect
but what other way
through the dark of the book
thinking how shall I lifeless murmur
the crushed past here beneath deepest seams
the underworld stroked and strophed to a stop
take these burnt essay's vowels
to illumine naked Ionian agonies
undarkened into form
O once bright beings
O dead
O passages of mine not mine
but who knew you would bring this commerce
this going back and forth
making crops grow
and die and
for god sakes grow again

Let the coal come out on its own two feet
their tools under
their arms

        'another way of paying us less!'
            vanishing
              mirth
      the life of the Underworld now
        rumbling round them

fissures   chirping   informers

    like miners attempting unions in lightless
        conversations
    like stones found to contain fires unactualized
    like word-ore decontextualized
    like the deep pockets time has for its hostages
    like a sexy pickaxe swing
    like light headed gas prophecies of spectral Communism
    like how much cash I can pull in
    like mine shafts flooded hidden abandoned still there
        like memory beneath calm city surfaces today

To undercut
    the Company's power

without speaking

Otherwise
    others
        folded

    just
        his voice   the
    a ledger   garden
        of water

                              a
                       station

                       She

                       whose

                       grocery

                       we owed
                       and they

                       never did

        Working in the mines   lit up
      down in something ages nobody knows
  the wonder   how came grandfather the time
        to sink shafts into dreaming

anger   guilt
(not poetic enough) — mere shovels:
                shovel rock
                shovel death
                shovel shit
                shovel breath

     sink
         their
     degeneration
underfed and spurting
       full of
         love

            The ideal
              voice
            swelling
              (writing)
              for that men pay
           until a miner earn
             enough   coal
           blazing a sort of
              suffering must
              engender retribution

Strike!

'Come on, friends, an' let's go down,
let's go down, let's go down,
come on, friends, an' let's go down,
down on the picket line!'

'the need to stay and put right what was wrong'   by February
1877 the first Wellington strike was on   never recognized as such
by Dunsmuir   who   Pluto in the dark century   replaced
'absent' workers with imported strike-breakers

'the baker was warned to bake us no bread and the butcher to
supply us no beef'   while at the tea party   the lawns
whale oil lamps clean of coal   Robert laughed a rare Scots
moment counting and cold   dreamt Scrooge of this tale
this simple explanation 'that no side is to blame for the hopeless
situation springing from the inevitable tragedy of life'
capital   competition   grocery list   industrial crisis

then evictions   miner's wives with babes in their arms hounding
strike-breakers at the mine gate   Lt. Colonel C.F. Houghton
(Victoria) and the Corps of Victoria Rifles   'one armed man for
every striking miner'   a sullen group watching the train pull into
Wellington   May 1877   'under the guise of maintaining
order'   under the gaze of Dunsmuir   conspiracy and black
gold   after four months   it is broken

Cumberland   1912   and spreading   a velvet line of miners
sweeping the open and muddy street (passing the general store my
ancestor looked out of?) with linked arms   and the gossamer of
their singing voices ascending the air tubercular in smoke rings of
dissent   dangling above the slag heap smoulder forming the
word 'scab' above their hatless heads Ginger marching the ghosts of
Étienne, Souvarine, fictional   marching to SCAB SCAB SCAB
SCAB

'These purse-proud aristocrats refuse to allow their miners to work
for a living wage'   a younger Dunsmuir now the target who but
evil personified can we place at the scene of the crime?

Plutarch   'one cannot much approve of gaining riches by
working mines   the greatest part of which is done by malefactors
and barbarians   mere criminals   some of them too
bound and perishing   in those close and unwholesome places'
the attitude as old as you want to imagine the breaths and deaths of
brigands much the same

The Company   coursing through Island trees   counting
coup   The Company   opposed to unions   undercutting
labour costs   on the backs of Chinese   Japanese   Italian
immigrants   The Company   feeling Gas Committees
(formed from miner's ranks)   interfered with production
safety a too costly measure   to be overlooked for efficiency's sake
sweet moneychanger   The Company profits from explosion
expatriation   export

June 1912   two Gas Committee members   tinkering with
sounds seams make   report gas in Extension #2   highly
volatile bituminous coal   are fired   LAUNCHED INTO
ETERNITY   by the daemonic blast   one of the two
Oscar Mattishaw   UMWA union man   known 'trouble
maker'   moves on to Cumberland 'to beard the lion'   the
next day   the daemonic blast of the Long Strike was on
disguised as a union declared 'holiday'   met with lockout
strike-breakers   constables with three-foot long
clubs   endless days of nothing but potatoes

For thirty days   the Boss Whistle blew each morning at the mine
no union man answering   watching from windows the backs of
those who did answer   black and bent

The Gas Committee

Listening to the two voices
discernible in the coal:
one barely overheard   barely
understood   filtered through the
layers of the yet unlit black rock

     the other
a naked flame lit
close by the ear
ready to hiss   fire   bang   crash

throw bodies into stark relief

open the earth to the sky

Little brick
to keep out   the open spaces (alive)

    devastated
by winter (by wages)   a few clumps
        chimneys (slag fires)

the heavy grey air (penniless)   this village like a mourning

       red tiled

There stood a group (crumpled)   by the Company dubbed
the wry humour of the poor

    knowing
no purpose   pressed   swollen

      the greasy steel cables flying through the air like inked
ribbons (writing fire trouble strike don't give in)

      everything

   a sudden silence

a moment murmured

(to come to this   angry and milling)

(to come to   one more cup of coffee   and the road)

She   old mother
Revolutionary Fury
man's death
boxes getting bigger
the injunction
against extraneous words
ignored
sure, everything was
a certain mirror
as they   opposite
looked at life
in such filth
as if you knew

the singing girls

'This is not a fight for a living
but for the right to live'

Profit
flies bellowing
Pound's Usury
on the bosses
wandered   rested
wise virtues
dirty bottoms
unrestrained
now both lodger
and ledger sleep
through the record
of who did what
for how much to whom

Furniture is sold   people starve   turn to their neighbours
their chickens   my grandmother's family lived on nothing but
potatoes   no loaves   butter   coffee   chicory   leeks
thought of the brioche   mush and beans   junk coal stolen
from the slag heap for a little heat in the damp shacks on Striker's
Beach (Union Bay)   'the man who goes to work tomorrow is a
SCAB'   May Day 1913

> *'I hate the company bosses,*
> *I'll tell you the reason why*
> *They cause me so much suffering*
> *And my dearest friends to die.*
>
> *These mighty company bosses,*
> *They dress in jewels an' silk*
> *But my darlin' blue-eyed baby,*
> *She starved to death for milk.'*

A bust-up   street thugs from   Vancouver and Victoria Italian
strike-breakers   not told they were strike-breakers   special
constables gleefully busting heads   scab   scab   scab
scab   scab   scab   scab   scab   scab

'They had a heck of a splatter!'
'Tending and mending way back in your mind'   1912/13
      'thirty graves all new dug in a row waiting the endurance
            to be filled'

Hot riots in the Summer of 1913   time asks who is the
      Archmanipulator?

A crowd
of union men
gathered before
Nanaimo's Princess
Theatre to hear
speeches —
The Archmanipulator!
when twelve constables
on horseback
rode in on them

In Cumberland
it was because of Cave
intent on clearing
the street of strikers
sweeping down on horse
back with clubs aloft —
The Archmanipulator!

War   scabs in the mine and woods   strikers erupting on the
streets before mines in Extension   Cumberland   Nanaimo
the chase   the battle   loot   smash   our history holler
smash   scab   scab   scab   scab   scab

(Where is my family
in this din   this echo
of time's prison cell?)

Hundreds gathered outside Number 1   deafening noise
and shouting din of pots and pans   police en
gulfed by the whelming crowd's anger   come up you
bloody scabs   from the mine hiding behind our coal
come up   and get your medicine

(Were we scabs
or union men?)

           'Where the Hell You Goin' '

           A mother dark and Victorian
           arrives fresh from England to
           claim her drowned son's body
           the middle of the riots and here's
           these English guys with suitcases
           whom the strikers would take
           to be scabs skulking along
           the Black Track towards South
           Wellington were it not for the
           escort of Big Louis Nuenthal and the
           scalding tongue of 'Mother England'

I belong to
Glasgow, dear
Old Glasgow Town
There's somethin'
The matter with
Glasgow
For it's goin'
Roun' an' roun'

                        The Company
                    overworked
        his mute   ferocious black beard
                        a thunderous
                Achilles
                spleen

                            pouring
                    that sort of thing
                        on the bosses'
                arrival   Desirée
                            looking to dodge
                moments   time
                having agreed   to conclude
        anxious   she found
                him a nuisance   upon
            her shoulders

With beams black the flying dust shutters continual   tubs of
        coal marrow tips hoppers armed with shovels   political
discussions   clenched teeth   straight down

I'm only
A common working man
As anyone can see
But when I'm drunk
on Saturday night
Glasgow
Belongs to me!

                The Company   told thousands
        of perks   You have coal   rattled length
        underneath   stayed with panic

Axelson in jail   his wife   a huge Swedish woman with a
man's bashed in hat   arrived at the back door (riot in Ladysmith
too) of the jailhouse with an axe in her hands   I guess the police
figured she meant business   they let Axelson go and then the
two of them   big Mrs. Axelson and little Mr. Axelson   led
the crowd of miners back to the strike-breaker's lodgings at the
Temperance Hotel

                    Once again   heaviness   black
           velvet night a large cellar   the Lady
           Morning   the Lady Coal   given
           wages to offer isolation   'we are   rents
           the ground   into balance   here   a
           land ladies   the amusement of the poor'

McKenzie heard a noise   hiss of gas rock tumble   and
rushed into the bedroom   night a riot of voices   scab
scab   scab   he picked up the dynamite and threw it at the
window   (the Company   made of glass)   but it bounced
right back at him (damn good glass!)   a curl of fire drawing an
arc above the eye   he picked it up again but the explosion
LAUNCHED INTO ETERNITY   his hand off one eye
and mashed him against the wall dramatic and narrative   bones
of the earth exposed

'If you ever come back to the Island
we'll kill every damn one of you'
disheveled and battered
like quick words   nineteen men
waited one long hour
a black list composed
Big Louis took up his position
at the door as his fellows
herded the scabs and strike-breakers
captured   the train at Nanaimo
a few minutes later disgorged
a subdued group of men
having drained them of everything
as they marched towards
the CPR dock
about 500 miners
quietly pushing them back in line

We have left the pits   and shall not go back down
the miner's voices in chorus its gold and embroideries
for my mother to mend a confused argument against
themselves in this hot-house atmosphere of Summer
1913 led by 'detestable agitators' or good friends with
good ideas

But for a glorious music   *'I saw one man playing a piano with*
     an axe'

Quickly nauseated by the reek of poverty
murmured the lady
to give   respectfully
nothing to capital
the same shattered body
leaning once again into the pick strike
at the coal face
such a pretty nobody
glancing at our mining village
to have a look at astonishment
going to sleep

                        The dark expression
                                inspired
                groups   dirty nosed
                peeping in the gardens
                                and the talk
                        like dry leaves
                twenty women listening

Who was   an onlooker   to shut out daylight   swollen to a
final explosion   shouting   full revolutionary upheaval
colliers soaking wildly through a cry   work appearing wet scurry
to fluster   the exodus to Extension   the crowd coming down
the hill   they brought in the militia   put an end to it at gun
point   'You are an enemy of the state'   'No   I am an
enemy of *all* states'   trials and blacklists   my ancestors sent
wandering   (part of me hopes)   by 1914   war having its
economic effects   war as an economic effect   work resumed

Souvarine

Though living   flashed
dug a field down
        the evenings

deathly still friendship seemed
the miners

lived for a tunnel under danger
penniless and blacklisted
        a foreigner

during a labour shortage   his employers
        quoted him as an example

every night his gaze   smoked
interminably   about the

groping space   whilst untiringly
all his rebellious instincts

threw him into the struggle of labour
against capital
        workers rising

fires rising in four corners of cities
'mow people down

wipe everything out   and when nothing
whatsoever is left
        of this rotten world

perhaps a better one will spring up'
such was Souvarine
        like a pose

common sense did not bother information
the oil lamp smoked a furnace of woe

by general fire (strike)   'there will have to be
another bust up'

'yes'   the molten plates to lick
'anarchy   the end of everything

    the whole world bathed in blood
    and purified by fire

    then we shall see'

    a vision

Étienne

Everyday   camped out broken seam
his course   the whole pit

was conversation
subsided

     began to quarry about
with fixed study
     the shifty nature of the rock

the narrow hardness of the coal
angrily   Étienne had business

a wave of the hand   some day
though waking the masters

an instinct to rebel   why poverty
ground
     the fact

corresponding for books a frenzy of
enthusiasm

     political economy
killing mining communities   co-operative
     work possessed his thinking

stage of constructing a system from reading
practical demands
     transformed

you were born in coal
hacked away ideas

his eyes and ears still tell him light from
dark waking   like good seed springing up

the old order jumbling
up his odd bits of reading

hesitating to embark
into certain knowledge non

existent   a universal kiss he took
of recalcitrant employers and bourgeois

miraculous believers in
a perfect society

visualized motionless
suddenly fallen back into the mire of

subterranean Orpheatic adventures
listening to Her sleep
     the support of miners from all the pits

the writing   a slow transformation
to the surface
     Étienne

tasting the joy   of silent October
alleging

Émile

The very idea of a mine
the drama of rock drilling
tortuous dark passages
of a half column grey, close set type
as light dissected by Impressionists
sweet on optic urgency

Émile, staring
into the grey pane of glass
'a corner of nature seen through a temperament'
enclosed by detached observation
a pattern of details
gallery of word pictures
as at the *Salon des Refusés*
the reviled, misunderstood, persecuted
become a hero and an inspiration

What Naturalism is there
in this dream world
of memory's art and architecture
and time's carefully orchestrated
anarchism?

Émile, whispering
to the subterranean miner
that works in us all —
            whither leads this shaft?

Ginger

He looks like pictures of my grandfather
both Englishmen, red heads, miners

for a time

he pauses in this poetry
dusted with coal on his ill fitting clothes
and his ill breathing lungs

the dark wall of fir and cedar dripping above
the dark wall of the coal seam sweating below

a frail man kneeling in the lightless pinch
of this frigate earth ballasted with bones of miners
crawling to cut the pressed life of tree's ancestors

'is Ginger the sort of fuel you use   to kindle
a fire in this shivering cannibal life   what the devil
is Ginger   sea-coal?   fire-wood?   lucifer

matches?   what the devil is Ginger?'
organizing for the union
striking coal   the Company   compassion

a clarion call

blacklisted   I wonder
did my grandfather know him
hear the frail freckled voice underground

blacklisted   did he travel with him
to Trail on their *Tah-ye-ta-bits*

did one of mine hear the gunshot
that took him down in the
Cumberland woods

down in time's own abandoned mine?

Shaft

Four

Invocation

You will come out
of some dark place
dreaming union
and purposeless peace

You will afford
occasions and prompt
opportunities   rocks lit
to light the heart's heat

You will fend off
imperfections

You will find me at
the scale's end writing
charting the black
path of your transports

You will find being
and becoming
a charge in words
laying vowels out
like iron filings

You will force the issue

You will breathe
damp morning air
free of coal dust

You will breathe   again
aforementioned
      a tissue in the tumult

Tenebrae

I have only this moment's sweet expanse to trouble time, to brush
against you, the undulating contours of eternity's sensate skin, a
shimmering veil or fabric of mind and memory I imagine rolling
from the great bolt in my heart across spaces history has traveled
oceans rivers mountain ranges to rake the coals of the past a little
closer and be warmed by them   O matrix of my making in and
amongst words I have only inherited   and I have only inherited
words   not who spoke them   not what they may have meant,
robbed as I am of context and propinquity I come fumbling towards
the light   towards the dark   a shovel full of breathlessness in
each wind blast of the ferry deck crossing coal for eyes and coal in
my chest you are shibboleth I love to re-dream   momentum
desire   the warmed tone my body moves in, poems through
which we are amused to imagine meaning passing clear and poems
dark and earthen presenting the opaque fact of their arbitrary word-
ness; yes poem I write to the moon new risen above shorn
silhouette of spruce and fir coastline looming adjacent this unblem-
ished sentence's unfolding towards its period.

I have undergone insurrections   underminings of my memories
intrusions of cryptic dark silences into those few places lit by the
mind   I have heard misfortunes call me to their succor   strike
the dark rock with their heavy spades sending sparked word's light
into the meaningless black earth   I have come from beyond the
word's shadow where there is nothing to remark   I have bathed
in the secondary light of the word and seen the scarlet mote unre-
membered in its fast flaming eye   and I was afraid of their
intentions and the authorship of ancestors begging my readership
write

Disaster

Down
with
    the
hidden
air

a sacred procession
of the slag heap establishment

Without
    the mind
factories,
the promiscuity of poverty
surprising

some
dandelions

Next day
  in the pit
existence
    seemed
      broken
dreaming
    a tunnel
recovered

by fire
barefoot

winging their black and silent course
    amid   clanging signals
    shouted orders
    resounding

The daylight
    fell like a stone into a well

'The constant spectre of widowhood'   He   not thinking
about possible accidents   living in fire damp   the lamps pale
and blue   a miner's ear to the dark seam listening to the little
noises therein   rock fall   the earth itself   out rages
May Day   1887   explosion at the recently opened #1,
Nanaimo   148 men killed walled live into the mine *Fortunado*
writing farewell messages in the dust on their shovels   as they
prepared to sleep   the long sleep LAUNCHED INTO
ETERNITY the *Colonist*'s headline read

and then the monotonous groaning went on guiding the men in
their   work   'A fall! Quick! Quick!'   they tumble to
common impulse   ensued in single file as though at the cut face
plunged down   fear   shone in the dark   their brother's
lamps bobbing the passages   galloping they reached the others
ventilation   felt there   sleep   without his lamp   some
evil   precious   bodily origins   the mysterious reverting to
its animal source

An enormous body of coal lifting ancient compressed dreaming
under Nanaimo   pierced with a vast network of tunnels and
slopes   seven miles of passages   stretching out under the
harbour the sea   out under Protection and Newcastle Islands
underwater underworld topographies named for convenience
Killeen Incline   *Big Incline*   *Spears & Lambs*   *Cobble
Hill*   *Puyallup*   a maze tapping three seams   Wellington
Newcastle   Douglas   this underworld   this Hades
filled with tapping   with bodies gasping   the press of stone
collapsing on dark lungs digging

One man alone and lampless   beneath Protection   the other
side of the fall breathing only the dead in the dark surround   'as
soon as the debris is cleared'   but there is no one alive to clear
it   this Orpheus alone unable to see and without animals to
charm singing to himself   without love following unseen
behind walking back alone in the dark   through old connecting
webs of passages   from Protection   back to little known
connections to #1 and then hopefully up into the town   if he
can recall remember recollect

Imagine   one man alive and alone in the vast infernal network
of the dead   his hands blind on copper trolley wire   striking
his hatless head   his dry fish oil lamp dangling   reading the
invisible signs the architectural braille of impossible textual mazes
hundreds of feet of stone above   and fish and boat bottoms
above that   Is this *Killeen?*   This *Spears & Lambs?*   His
memory a blueprint structure of spaces containing images of escape
daylight   the beauty   of time wasted

some door   framed   the yard   beyond light
the chill days of November desired
the night   like a shroud
                the ashen sky
                her paintbrush touching a star above

I Will Imagine Ancestors I Cannot Know

She would have come from
Newcastle in black Victorian dress
unsuited to sea crossings, her
box of brushes and paints, two
stretched canvases awaiting sea blue
sagging with the moisture of six
weeks of Atlantics.

She would have arrived in a
shuddering cart clattering on a
rutted road, dusted from the dirt,
at her husband's cedar shack
backed by endless sea green forest.

She would have been sick for a time
and the fear of losing her kept
the house dark bolted and immobile,
unpainted, unimagined.

After weeks she would have emerged
cleaning and ordering, eyeing the
forest mists and the cinder path to the
mine her husband walked with others
similarly black faced singing and unknown.

She would have begun painting
the dark after a time,
taking charcoal
from her husband's face
running her fingers across

paper contours looking
for the lines, seams of
the impossibility of fire
illuminating the inside of
dark intricate images

the glitter of ghosts of trees
lurking outside in black shadow.

She would have taken fire.

She would have burned, lingering
in the dark wood's texture, led deep
into the underneath by the channels
of sweat lining her husband's coal
dusted body, run-off, tailings, gash vein

coming up out of the unlight
into root earth she paints with water
for hair darting dark with sea
birds diving sleek unseen movements

awake on a seam between breaths
into the refractions of her painting
one tumbling world into the next

willing him home and alive.

Imagining Ancestors

He groped the dark remembrance
        branchings of seam gaps
in stone lurching beneath fish
        and coal dark prospects
as in the night enclosed
        living room
one will move slowly recollecting where
        the chair legs are
        the coffee table
        the door jamb
only here
        the room is not for living and
        the dark is endless after
explosions of silence and ear damage
        ringing him through
the ugly underground of memory
        wandering strip shaft
hanging wall
        ground sluice
soft plate
        his memorial glossaries unfold

A hunger for light
leads his way
flume fuse and gash vein
        He remembers
stories — the swindler who led tours of
        closed mines
to show the curious 'the Devil himself
        in His Infernal magesty'
He remembers
        the shape of his architectural
escape

Imagining stars
in the dark solidity above —
mica flecks?
Phosphorus in the seabed
flooding above the
translucent tunnel shafts?
Flakes of coloured light in the painted
superstructure imprisoned

Would he — he was an educated man —
would he have read
his Ruskin?
The sublimity of the black
vastness
shadow employed only
to make the contours
felt throughout
while in *this* dark
the 'Parasitical Sublime':
where features are used
for the sake of the shadows
his ancestral mind actually lifting
Lamps of Architecture from the night:
Lamp of Sacrifice
Lamp of Truth
Lamp of Power
Lamp of Beauty
Lamp of Life
Lamp of Memory
Lamp of Obedience

He would have had to have come up
out of the dark beneath

for there to have been
        a family following

His memory providing soft *loci* and sharp image
        an Art of Memory
as his art of escape:
        bore hole (a clear glen)
drop shaft (antlers at the Temperance Hotel)
        flouting (the sea at night)
foot wall (her auburn hair)
        reef wash (the dock at Troon)
This is not difficult
the copper essence of night
she paints helping his escape
sienna umber veridian
brushing him up out of the ground
grit in the oil
horse haired from the green

Invocation

Moving through the heavy
u n light   labour pains
the pulse of   s u b terranean
traffic   the lines of air
leaching out under
the harbour's waters
this is the remembered
u n remembered   the sightless
shafts of family forming
duration's own slag heap
growing on the outskirts
of place
        no cool dark
u n rest   no labour
finished   they rise
as the blackest rye bread rises
from pans of caramelized words
prepared for placing them in

this jet piece of my body

this   u n lit looking back

Ferry glide. Harbour dock. Rental car. Kenning my way into clear Autumn Nanaimo day. The town's escarpment of sandstone jutting like an open jaw mouthing upward, forested mountains backing up behind coastal plain, sky of lurking October blue, casting light and shadow about as rubble from a luminaristic avalanche. I envision ancestors hacking clearings out of the green. A bastion. A coal dock and slag heap no longer in evidence. My car parked outside the museum, gravel footsteps above all the cavernous passageways carved out silent abandoned there still beneath this moving city surface, this glassy harbour, decades of silence and decay collapsing beneath. In the archive it doesn't take long to find the names in the ledgers and lists — Kirkwood, Saunders, Willey. But there is little else, no elaboration, few details, faint candlelight carried into the cathedraled dark. These were poor digging folk choking on coal dust: history does not record their eventful days. I must sink memory mines into the unknown, going on gossip and family hearsay. I drive into Wellington where they lived. What remains? Strip mall. Shallow lake. Marsh land. The original dwellings were disassembled and carried south to Extension, following Dunsmuir's hot pursuit of the subterranean Black Track. I don't know if any of mine moved there too. I think most stayed behind when the mining moved on, finding new work under better lighting. Shift gears and bear down. This is the matrilineage. But the patrilineage — and somehow this figures — some records remain in the Cumberland archives (moving north on the Island). Shop keeper. Town father. Managerial class. Until my grandfather refused to spy for the company and took up the pick with the labouring others. How I romance this history, kenning my way, sinking small shafts of light — pinholes really — into the dark of our history here.

Memory Mine I

Spinning
end over end
in the endless
night
canine
Cerberus
cerebral
my grandmother's
voice
arcing out from
the tape recorder
quavers
a bad boy
once dropped
a small dog
down one of the
abandoned
mine shafts
listening
to the electric
crackle
and static
of its barks
echoing
up sounding
the depths

I haunt Museums and small Island towns of former life. I finger old fading newspapers and arcana of turn of the century photographs. There are reports on the qualia of the upper classes that do not exist for those labouring beneath ground, their architectures described because where they are from 'everyone owns the residence in which he lives.' At some point, poised with hands on steering wheel, the car rolling over a hill into view of the town and the silver finned harbour, I find myself saying this, turning the dark echo over and over, bad photocopies of photographs on the seat beside me, saying this, that time turns back and bites its serpentine tail, that coming here hopeful I re-enact their passage a hundred years before, that I am inevitably my great grandmother's dreams of the yet to be painted, my great grandfather's fear of the cramped and pressing dark shortening his speech into monosyllabic stutter.

It is Toussaint now, November 1st, day to remember the dead, putting pieces of them back together as they crowd forward from the night before accomplices in a shadow nocturn the delight of limits and barely made out whispers. The day says poems so I write flames of people are leaves falling this autumnal escape each dead bud broken on sidewalks seems sleepier than the last O spring your heart is the echo of silent leaf drift a moment to pour lyric license onto early light and shadow. Your own ochery image stalls against the wall before you can walk out imagined and have the wind replace your breathing. Scant memory makes me write clearly so I will for now be to the point.

Memory Mine II: Hello Dolly!

Sea crossings
mind and hand filled
with silver fins
scales of the tenuous
darting dark
to Rivers Inlet
cannery
(silver fins filling
silver tins)
the bare cedar shack
and their pet
bear Dolly found
a foundling
on the shore who
when sick
of salmon they one
day ate, my
great grandfather
worried over
his son's sadness at
a devoured pet
but the boy simply
wiped his chin
and asked for more
Dolly.

Memory Mine III

A pirouette
in the dark
small hands holding
her father's grey
work shirt shifting
down the Model T
turns following
the lightless
seam from Nanaimo
to Coalmont down
the cinder road
out of work again
(blacklisted)
going south 'to where
the oranges grow'
her father
grinning sunward
daughters clustered
on the back seat
crying they came
close before
the car turned north
again
the coal tunnels
funneling them back
along
California highways
naked lights
descending again

into dank B.C. shafts
of colourless dust
and debris
outcast but without
escape.

Memory Mine IV

You are feeding
the feeling, the fire

The old man stripping down
by the tin tub
in the kitchen, colour of
an olive, the deep pits of
his eyes looking at his
last day of work
his retirement his death
in black rivers on his flesh

You don't get outside
the dark shaft, the
endless shift

My grandmother, fourteen
feeds the fire in the
schoolhouse she no longer
attends with coal from
the scuttle — she likes
horses and a train hand
named Ernest
shuttling cars filled with coal

Her father, stooping still
in the shafts under
her feet, looking into

the dark infinity
of the day he will die
in a bath on the day
he retires from the mine.

'I Gave Turtle Island to Someone and did not Get It Back'

Fled
      this thought

its own politics torpor

      bemoan
   aquifer
   articulations

percolating to the page

unsettling settlers / appropriating appropriators

    I love them, the
    avenging heroes now being dreamt up;
    I hate them, the
    angry haters themselves discriminating
    and discriminated against —

in this language a shaft falling

to speak being from been
to becoming

every text an amanuensis
calling down time

    What does one do
    with one's survivor guilt? All history
    is survivor guilt.

moments I am thrown into

becoming ancestral

They were Labour's heroes and angry bigots
at once — locked
in unlit enclosures of context   place
time   demographics
hating everything unfamiliar dirty   dark
enclosed in mind
tongues lashing spitting familial into
new worlds with axes
picks and centuries of cultural baggage mixing.

    A people
who wherever they went they ripped up
Eden solid rock trees
animals anything emigrating into view.

    A people
who have taken burdening themselves with
time's slow fingered thefts
as I have taken word (fire)   mine
not mine   speaking
the stolen language we all pilfer each other's
ears with

but guilt stands
in the way of responsibility.

Let me speak (write)
clearly: I love them, avenging heroes,
I hate them
angry pick swingers, the dark home
to inexhaustible resources
of history's yet unrealized unfoldings

Inheritance and
Poetry   the black lump inside the body
beating me down and
bearing me up

In Cumberland the dwelling of H.P. Collis is still 'assuming propor-
tions' of recollection (driving / another town clinging to the green
beyond) 107 years later — 'a character house representing no partic-
ular school, but rather its owner' (a piece of the fortune / piece of
time). Old empty rooms to place candles to remembering, images
of lives led despite the fact that 'the divisions at present indicate but
little the use of the various rooms.' I place the counters where I will
in this forgotten ancestral home — a woman gathering her children
for the crossing back to England to spend three years there
'educating them' — the quiet that follows as the one man alone
observes 'the best art of the past married to the present' in the garish
faux fixtures of the period — a pipe cooling atop a catalogue after
his return from California (for what purpose — to assess the market
for coal for the owners of the earth?) — coal barons dropping in
(need I fear and imagine this?) to complain of labour unions, lazy
workers, shifty Chinese (slurs I hope falling on the deaf ears of the
town shopkeeper) — but I do not know what really raged in these
now decaying rooms, described in the WEEKLY NEWS as 'so cozy, so
spacious, so unique,' I do not know, I recollect, piece by tiny piece,
not sure why I want to know which side we were on, labour and
capital two poles stretching out time, the uneven contours of cast
shadow and made light reconfiguring another context.

Memory Mine V

Four figures stand before
the Big Store
Cumberland, 1894
a gaze time does not return —
it is the aporia of
time's tinkering thought

How do you manage
so many goods
(you cannot count the evils
in tins and flour sacks)?
*Gents' Furnishings, Boots
& Shoes, Groceries,
Hardware & Furniture,
Wine, Whisky & Gin* —

The only store in a
coal grey town
and one of those four
in the photograph
is my great grandfather
staring out at the street
on which the heads of union
men were clubbed by constables
in the long strike of 1912-14

How do you manage
the goods of the intellect
the goods of the body's labours
the goods some say are gods
tokens to be taken
but never bought and owned?

The saving grace is this story —
the shopkeeper's son
sent by Dunsmuir into the mine
as a spy to report on
the voice of underworld agitation
could not
and took up the pick and shovel instead
to labour
labour
moving down into the dark
stuttering shell shock of war

The goods were what he turned
down   his escape
leaves his skin white beneath
the black film
his memory reeling — forever a catacomb
of lightless Piranesi nightmares
his voice a stutter
of coal rock collapse

After his long walk
through the painted dark underworld alone
(not a *Heurtebise* in his imagination)
he mined no more
took to the air to fight a war
took to ship and sea
to be above always above
what might tinker dark and unseen
beneath

However true,
however false,
it's this illumines
the dark figures photographed
before the dim store.

Scars

Pinpoints of
purple light

the graft of
given form

here an arrow
entered slaying

empire here
Thomas inserted

his finger
doubting Christ

zones more Gothic
than temptation

soft corpuscular
scarlet seraphs

obtaining delight
in lesion

Obliterate

legions

of perfect

cells

here

it is written

Manolo

fell

from his

bike

taking

knee

Surgery carves
time an insignia

this blood mark
man made and

signifying only
other scars

skin text tissue
without reference —

there is no
pre-scar life

we can return to —
we are born in scar

navel fontanelle
birthmark bloodied

Identification

is injury

purple

with

birth

white

with

age

a ribbon

crosses

thigh

revealing

Odysseus'

long

awaited

return

The nipple
>(not a scar
>you are mistaken)

The orifice
>(yes given scars
>that are centres
>of pleasures burst)

The mouth
>(horizontal
>gash
>bleeding
>language)

The wrinkles
>(time scars
>the eyes toward
>sightless distances)

The mouth
>(yes
>the cut kiss
>breath
>utterance hurts)

The wrinkles
>(crease between
>seams and
>seems — laughs
>tears portraits)

Cheating severity's
ghost Thyestes

stares at his plate
fingering his knife hilt

half of life is
scarred over

tissue the other
half is still bleeding

each lesion a
lesson in how to

bear the blows
being dealt —

feathers iron
cross stitch and canoe

Tailings: What Remains

What remains

animal particle

these words

ceaselessly

prefatory

lamps held into

the dark

inverted

architecture

of coal mines

and forgotten time

Only

a heap

of unsorted

molecula

strophing

its lexical

ghost

mountain

of detritus

unshorn

outside

the curve of

town time

This is

the wreck of

identity's

rhetoric

a lit self

sudden

against

opaque

other

belied by

the fact

that all

is mezzo

and drifting

between

wrecks

The past is

is not

what we are

remains

antechamber

entered

the extremity of

history's

becoming

a building

time topples

and builds toward

again

I would like to thank the editors of the journals in which sections of *Mine* have appeared: *Dandelion*, *Stuffed Dog*, and *Van*. Thanks also to Rob Clark and Low Fi Press for printing material from *Mine* in the chapbook *The Preface* (Low Fi 2001). Special thanks to the Cumberland Museum and Archives for their kind assistance and generosity. I would also like to thank Lisa Robertson, Roger Farr, Steve Ward, Jordan Scott, and Reg Johanson for their support, friendship and willing ears. Thanks to Josh and Hannah for keeping things light, and to my sister Gail Tulloch for years of encouragement. Thanks also to my colleagues and students at Simon Fraser University.